A Salute to Historic Black Educators

Copyright © 1990, 1996 by Empak Publishing Company

ISBN 0-922162-14-X (Volume X)
ISBN 0-922162-15-8 (Volume Set)

A Salute to Historic Black Educators

EMPAK PUBLISHING COMPANY

Publisher & Editor: Richard L. Green
Senior Editor: Sylvia Shepherd
Researcher: Sylvia Shepherd
Production: Dickinson & Associates, Inc.
Illustration: S. Gaston Dobson
Preface: Empak Publishing Co.

When you consider that, during the days of slavery, Black Americans were forcibly denied the rights of obtaining an education, the dedicated and determined men and women presented in this book standout like educational giants. Many of the individuals reported upon were sons or daughters of former slaves, while others were actually born slaves.

In colonial days, it was against the law for slaves to learn to read and write. It was also against the law for any White to aid a slave in gaining an education. Any open teaching of slaves ended after slave revolts frightened slave owners, who saw education as a real threat to the institution of slavery. It was reasoned that by keeping slaves uneducated, passive, and controllable, slave owners' investment in human lives and "free labor" would be preserved.

After the Civil War, opportunities for Blacks to obtain an education became somewhat more available. Missionaries and religious organizations established schools, and the education of ex-slaves began. Higher education for Blacks also started after the war, and in these pages you will often see mention of such pioneering colleges and universities as Howard, Fisk, Talladega, Morehouse, Virginia Union, Shaw, and Morgan State. Also presented is the rift that existed regarding the aims of a Black educational thrust: the vocational training supporters of Tuskegee and Hampton versus the advocates of academic education.

In *A Salute to Historic Black Educators*, you will meet Blacks who managed not only to gain an education while slavery existed, but also went on to become high achievers, who involved themselves with the education of a new generation of Blacks. You will read about scholars of Latin and Greek, formal holders of Phi Beta Kappa keys, presidents of colleges, and people of national reputation. You will meet Lucy Craft Laney, who begged and borrowed to help her students; William H. Crogman, who received no formal education until he was 25 years old; Benjamin E. Mays, who influenced the Rev. Martin

Luther King, Jr.; and Charles Spurgeon Johnson, who helped Japan reorganize its school system after World War II.

Empak is proud to add Volume X, *A Salute to Historic Black Educators*, to its series of Black history publications. Researching this book was a labor of love that revealed the magnitude of what an opportunity and education can offer. It also conveyed the vital importance of preparing oneself for a life of achievement and self-actualization.

Empak Publishing Company

Oops!

ERRATA: Biographies • Arthur S. Schomburg
• Booker T. Washington

Page <u>50</u> and <u>54</u>, PHOTO LINE DRAWINGS:
Biography photo line drawings should be interchanged.

CONTENTS

Editor's Note: Due to this booklet's space limitations, some facets on the lives of the above noted Blacks in Education have been omitted.

CHARLOTTE HAWKINS BROWN
(1883-1961)

Charlotte Hawkins Brown's determination was contagious. Her enthusiasm and dedication drew people to her. She inspired confidence with an aura of practical wisdom. With determination, she converted a run-down old church into a 300-acre campus called the Palmer Memorial Institute. Employing a variety of activities, she raised most of the school's funds personally.

Charlotte Hawkins was born in 1883 to Caroline Frances Hawkins and Edmund H. Hight, a brick mason, in Henderson, North Carolina. Charlotte never knew her father, therefore, she used her mother's maiden name. When Charlotte was about 7 years old, her mother took her to Massachusetts, where living conditions were better for Blacks. Charlotte blossomed in her new environment, showing enough early self-confidence and ability to be chosen speaker at her grammar school graduation ceremony in Cambridge, Massachusetts. She would later recall that these years were unscarred by racial prejudice. In fact, her high school principal remained a lifetime friend and supporter.

Although Hawkins hoped to attend Radcliffe College, a liberal arts school in Cambridge, she realized the practical advantages of becoming a teacher. So, she enrolled in Massachusetts State Normal School in Salem. It was at this point in her life that she met an influential mentor, Alice Freeman Palmer, President of Wellesley College in Massachusetts. It was Palmer who introduced Hawkins to people who could help her, and it was in honor of Palmer that Hawkins would later name her school.

The humble origins of Palmer Memorial Institute began in Sedalia, North Carolina, in 1902, one year after Hawkins' college graduation. It would remain under her leadership until 1952, and her financial direction until 1955. From a classroom in an old church and a dormitory in a log cabin, Palmer would grow to 14 modern buildings valued at more than one million dollars. This achievement was accomplished by aggressively soliciting the support of Blacks and Whites, both in the South and in the North. Major support was given, for example, by Black businesswoman Madame C.J. Walker, and the Julius Rosenwald Fund.

Palmer's preparatory school for girls stressed the importance of manners and culture in achieving racial progress. In pursuit of this, the school sponsored exchange programs with schools for young White women. Hawkins believed her school was one of the first places in North Carolina where the races could mingle.

In 1911, Hawkins married Edmund S. Brown. Although childless, they reared six children of relatives, including Charlotte Brown's niece, Maria, who later married Nat"King" Cole. To these responsibilities, Brown added to her own education. She studied at Harvard in Cambridge, Simmons College in Boston, and Temple University in Philadelphia. She received her college degree from Wellesley, where she was later elected an honorary member of the Wellesley College Alumnae Association.

Honorary degrees were awarded to Brown from North Carolina State College, Wilberforce University, Lincoln University, and Howard University. In addition to being an outstanding educator, Brown was a national women's leader. She was a founder of the North Carolina State Federation of Negro Women's Clubs, a Vice-President of the National Association of Colored Women, and President of the North Carolina Negro State Teachers Association.

Brown's belief that interracial contacts were necessary to advance the education of Black youths led her to become a founder of the Commission on Interracial Cooperation in 1919. Charlotte Hawkins Brown died on January 11, 1961, and financial difficulties closed Palmer Institute in 1971. But, Brown had left her mark on many Black women who benefitted from her crusade for "race pride, mutual respect, sympathetic understanding, and interracial goodwill."

HALLIE QUINN BROWN
(c.1845 - 1949)

In 1899, Hallie Quinn Brown, the daughter of former slaves, had tea with Queen Victoria at the Windsor Castle in England. She was the guest of the Lord Mayor of London and addressed the International Conference of Women there. It had been quite a journey for a European celebrity who once was a farm girl.

Hallie was born on March 10, 1845(?), in Pittsburgh, Pennsylvania, to Thomas Arthur and Frances Jane Brown, both ex-slaves. While Hallie was still small, the Browns took their six children to live in Chatham, Ontario, Canada, hoping the move to a farm would improve Mrs. Brown's poor health. Hallie received her early education in Canada, leaving in 1870 to enter Wilberforce University in Ohio.

By the time she received her bachelor's degree in 1873, the rest of the Brown family had moved to Ohio. While in college, Hallie heard a speech given by Susan B. Anthony, an early champion of women's equality, that caused her to become a crusader for women's voting rights. This would be the beginning of Brown's reputation as a suffragette.

After graduation, Brown moved south and taught school on plantations, and in the public schools of Yazoo, Mississippi, and Columbia, South Carolina. While in Columbia, she was Dean of Allen University, from 1885 to 1887. After moving to Dayton, Ohio, Brown operated a night school for southern migrants in addition to teaching school. In 1892, she returned south, for one year as Dean of Women at the Tuskegee Institute in Alabama.

During her early teaching years, Brown became interested in public speaking and graduated, in 1886, from the Chautauqua Lecture School. She soon became a popular public speaker in both northern and southern cities, from New York to Louisiana. In 1894, after accepting an appointment as a professor of elocution at Wilberforce University, Brown began touring Europe as a lecturer. Her visit with Queen Victoria occurred during one of these tours. During her travels, she raised funds for Wilberforce that paid for the Emery Hall dormitory on the campus. Typical of her lecture topics were "The Progress of Negro Education and Advancement in America Since Emancipation"; "The Status of the Afro-American Woman Before and After the War"; and the "Negro Folklore and Folksong."

After her European tours, Brown was an English instructor and trustee at Wilberforce University for many years. In 1900, she became active in the crusade for women's rights. She traveled extensively, speaking out for the full citizenship rights of women, and she also was an outspoken supporter of civil rights for Blacks. In 1925, upon discovering the segregated seating arrangements of Blacks by the International Council of Women, she lead a Black attendance boycott of the All-American Musical Festival in Washington, D.C.

Also active in politics, Brown campaigned on behalf of Warren G. Harding in 1920, the year that women were first allowed to vote. She also was a speaker at the Republican Party convention in 1924. From 1920 to 1924, she was President of the National Association of Colored Women, where she also founded and served as chairman of the Scholarship Fund. During her presidency, the association assumed the maintenance costs of the Frederick Douglass home in Washington, D.C.

Brown was the author of several books: *Bits and Odds, A Choice Selection of Recitations; First Lesson in Public Speaking; Machile; The African; Tales My Father Told; Our Women: Past, Present and Future; Pen Pictures of Pioneers of Wilberforce;* and *Homespun Heroines and Other Women of Distinction.*

On September 16, 1949, Hallie Quinn Brown died in Wilberforce of coronary thrombosis. This farm girl, whose birth year is not certain, used her talents to overcome obscurity and to achieve international recognition. Her entire adult life was spent as an educator, activist and bearer of the message of equality for all.

PETER HUMPHRIES CLARK
(1829 -1925)

Peter Humphries Clark, grandson of William Clark of the famous Lewis and Clark expedition, achieved fame as one of the leading Black educators of his day. He was also an early political activist, a mobilizer of the Black vote, and one of the first Black Socialists in the United States.

Peter Humphries Clark was born in Cincinnati, Ohio, around 1829, to Michael Clark, son of Lt. William Clark. Lt. Clark, a slave owner, who lived near Lexington, Kentucky, and fathered five children by his mulatto slave, Betty. Fearing he might die during the expedition, Lt. Clark resettled Betty and the children on free soil in Cincinnati. Michael, married an Irish-American woman, Ann Humphries, who became Peter Clark's mother.

Obtaining an early education was difficult for Peter, who did not want to become a barber like his father, Michael. His opportunity arrived in 1844, when the Rev. Hiram Gilmore opened a high school for Blacks. Peter's scholastic ability earned him a job as an assistant teacher while he was still a student. After leaving school in 1848, he apprenticed to a White printer, Thomas Varney, for more than a year. In 1849, when the Ohio legislature enacted a law allowing Blacks to organize and operate their own schools, Clark became a teacher. The prejudice he encountered so angered and disgusted him that he left for Africa in 1850.

After reaching New Orleans, however, Clark abandoned his emigration plans and soon returned to Cincinnati, where he became involved in politics and Black civic groups. In 1853, he was Secretary of the National Convention of Colored Men in Rochester, New York. That same year, he drafted the constitution of the National Equal Rights League, a Black organization.

In 1856, he joined the newly organized Republican Party and remained a member until 1872. Meanwhile, his Black interests and Unitarian religious beliefs were in conflict with the Cincinnati school board, and he left teaching. He opened a grocery store, later became editor of the *Herald of Freedom*, and then worked on the staff of Frederick Douglass' newspaper, the *North Star*.

In 1857, Peter Clark returned to teaching and eventually became principal of the new Gaines High School in Cincinnati, a job he held for 30 years. His students were in great demand as teachers, and Clark was respected for his honesty and high principles. During this time, Clark married Frances Williams, a music teacher and graduate of Oberlin College in Ohio. One daughter, Consuelo, studied both art and medicine. The Clarks' son, Herbert, became a deputy sheriff and a teacher.

Clark later became displeased with the Republican Party's indifference to the problems of Blacks. So, he became one the first Black Socialists in the United States. He joined the Workingman's Party of the United States and, in 1877, the party nominated him for Ohio State Superintendent of Schools. Although he lost the election, he fared much better than the rest of the ticket. Because of his Socialist activities, Clark was called an "agitator" by people who feared change. In 1887, he was removed from his teaching position because of his political activism.

Clark left Cincinnati and took a job as principal of the State Normal and Industrial School in Huntsville, Alabama. Unable to tolerate the segregation of the South, he went to St. Louis, where he taught in Black public schools until retiring in 1908. Peter Humphries Clark died on June 21, 1925, in St. Louis, at the age of 96.

Steadfast in his principles, Clark was frequently in conflict with the White establishment. He was sometimes called a radical, when actually he was ahead of his time. He willed his philosophy books to a St. Louis library and, as if to get in the last word, he willed his most beloved volumes - books of poetry by noted Black writers - to Cincinnati's Library.

RUFUS E. CLEMENT
(1900 - 1967)

In 1966, one of the 14 most influential university presidents in America was Rufus E. Clement of Atlanta University. This honor from Time magazine was a great tribute to Clement, a man who began early to make his mark as an outstanding achiever.

Rufus was born on June 26, 1900 in Salisbury, North Carolina, where his father, George Clinton Clement, was a minister and later Bishop of the A.M.E. Zion Church. In 1946, his mother, Emma Clarissa Clement, was the first Black woman to be chosen "Mother of the Year." Following in their parents' footsteps, all seven of the Clement children, including Rufus, attended Livingstone College in Salisbury. When Rufus graduated in 1919, he had earned three letters in athletics and was valedictorian of his class.

Clement went to Evanston, Illinois, where he enrolled in the Garrett Biblical Institute and Northwestern University. In 1922, he earned a Bachelor of Divinity degree from Garrett, and a Master of Arts degree from Northwestern. That same year, he returned to Livingstone College as a history instructor. After three years, Clement became a history professor and dean of the college, the latter appointment making him one of the youngest academic deans in the country. Under his leadership, Livingstone gained accreditation from the Southern Association of College and Secondary Schools.

Clement's interest in athletics continued, and he was the football coach at Livingstone. He also served as a football official for the Colored Intercollegiate Athletic Association and was a founder of the Midwestern Atlantic Association, for which he became commissioner. From 1929 to 1931, Clement also served as minister of the A.M.E. Zion Church in Landis, North Carolina, which was 17 miles from Salisbury. In 1930, he received his doctorate from Northwestern University.

In 1931, Dr. Clement became Dean of the new Louisville Municipal College, set up for Blacks in affiliation with the University of Louisville. Here, too, he brought the curriculum up to accreditation standards. In 1937, he was elected President of Atlanta University and began his 30 years as leader of that institution. During his tenure, the university opened a School of Library Science, a School of Education, and a School of Business.

In 1954, Dr. Clement became a member of the Board of Education in Atlanta, the first Black to serve on a major southern city's school board since Reconstruction. As a board member, serving 14 years, he developed a racial integration plan for the city's public schools. He also devoted time and effort to end discrimination and segregation in such areas as employment and voting rights.

Dr. Clement belonged to a wide variety of organizations, including the United Nations Association of America; the American Historical Society; the American Academy of Political Science; the National Science Foundation; the American Council on Education; and the Advisory Council on African Affairs of the U.S. State Department. In 1964, Clement was the official United State's representative at the ceremony marking the independence of the African country of Malawi.

Dr. Clement received honorary degrees from the University of Liberia, Virginia Union University, Manhattanville College in New York, and Virginia State College. In 1957, he became an honorary member of Phi Beta Kappa at the Brown University in Providence, Rhode Island. Dr. Rufus E. Clement died on November 7, 1967, while attending meetings of Atlanta University trustees in New York City. Surviving were his widow, the former Pearl Anne Johnson, whom he had married in 1919, and their daughter.

Just a year before Dr. Rufus Clement's death, *Time* magazine had chosen him as a national leader in education. The magazine had pointed to the two aspects of Dr. Clement's life in which he took particular pride amid his many accomplishments, "skill in race and human relations, first, and foreign relations, particularly African, second."

FANNY JACKSON COPPIN
(1837-1913)

Only $125 stood between Fanny Jackson and the freedom to become a great educator, lecturer, and missionary. But, in the 1840s that was a large sum of money. So large that the story of Fanny Jackson Coppin might only have been the birth, life, and death of a slave.

Fanny was born into slavery in 1837, in Washington, D.C. Although her grandfather purchased freedom for himself and four of his six children, he had not saved enough to also buy the freedom of Fanny's mother, Lucy. Fanny's aunt, Sarah Clark, however, looked at her little slave niece and saw potential. For almost two years, she worked for $6.00 a month to save the money ($125) to buy Fanny's freedom.

Once freed, Fanny was sent to live with another aunt in New Bedford, Massachusetts, and eventually went to work for the George Calvert family in Newport, Rhode Island. There, she received private lessons in the Calvert home and later attended a public school for Blacks. Fanny and Mrs. Calvert became very close friends.

However, Fanny was forced to leave Newport to seek further education. Years later, Fanny would write about her move to Bristol, Rhode Island, to attend the Rhode Island State Normal School: "I never would have left her (Mrs. Calvert), but it was in me to get an education and to teach my people. This idea was deep in my soul. Where it came from I cannot tell ... It must have been born in me."

In 1860, after completing her courses at Normal, Fanny entered Oberlin College in Ohio, where she studied Greek, mathematics, and French. Oberlin was a college far ahead of its time—the first coeducational college in the United States, and the first recognized college to admit Blacks. At Oberlin,

Fanny was able to live up to the expectations of her Aunt Sarah, who continued to give her financial support.

Fanny's accomplishments at Oberlin included becoming the class poet, the first black student-teacher, an organizer of an evening class to teach newly freed slaves, and a teacher of private music lessons. In 1865, at her graduation ceremonies, she read her essay in French.

After graduation, Fanny was immediately hired by the Institute for Colored Youth in Philadelphia. Four years later, she became its principal. Under her guidance, the school added classes to prepare students for the teaching profession. This program was so successful that the students were hired for jobs long before they graduated. She also added industrial training courses to prepare young Blacks for various trades. Jackson helped raise $17,000 for the Industrial Department by lecturing and organizing a trades fair.

In 1881, Fanny married the Rev. Levi J. Coppin, pastor of the Philadelphia Bethel Church. Although Rev. Coppin wanted his wife to give up teaching, she continued her work at the Institute for 19 years. She did, however, add church missionary work to her busy schedule.

In 1888, Fanny Coppin went to London as a delegate to an international conference on missionary work. Two years later, her husband was made a bishop in the African Methodist Episcopal Church and assigned to Cape Town, South Africa. In 1902, she joined him and entered into missionary work. With her customary energy, she organized temperance and missionary groups in Cape Town, and traveled throughout Africa setting up A.M.E. missions.

In 1904, the couple returned home to Philadelphia, where failing health eventually curtailed Fanny's many activities. Before her death from arteriosclerosis on January 21, 1913, Fanny Coppin wrote an autobiography, *Reminiscences of School Life, and Hints on Teaching.* In it, she advised teachers never to use the word dumb in a classroom and to be patient, wise, and skillful in dealing with children. "Remember," Coppin wrote, "... all the time you are dealing with a human being, whose needs are like your own."

JOSEPH C. CORBIN
(1833-1911)

Prior to the Civil War, when slavery prevented Blacks from obtaining an education, Joseph C. Corbin earned several college degrees and mastered Latin, Greek, German, French, Spanish, Italian, Hebrew, and Danish.

Corbin was born on March 26, 1833 in Chillicothe, Ohio. He was eldest son of 11 children born to William and Susan Corbin. After receiving a basic education in several small schools, he enrolled in Ohio University in Athens, obtaining a bachelor's degree in 1853, and a master's degree in 1856. After a brief period of working in a Cincinnati bank and then teaching school in Louisville, Kentucky, Corbin edited a Black newspaper in Cincinnati, *The Colored Citizen*.

In 1872, Corbin and his wife of four years, Mary Jane, moved to Little Rock, Arkansas and, like so many Blacks in the postwar South, joined the Republican Party. That same year, he worked as a reporter for the party newspaper, *The Daily Republican*, and was slated to run for state superintendent of schools that same year. In the election, he won by a small margin over the White incumbent, Thomas Smith. Corbin, however, never completed his term because he was removed by southern Democrats returning to power in 1874. Corbin then left Arkansas to teach at the Lincoln Institute in Jefferson City, Missouri.

When the liberal Democrats gained control of the trustee positions of Arkansas State University, they decided to open a branch for Blacks. Realizing that Corbin was the ideal candidate for this job, they lured him back to Arkansas. In 1875, in an old Civil War barracks, he established the Branch Normal College in Pine Bluff with only seven students. Later, Corbin prevailed upon the trustees for a larger, permanent school building. In 1883, the trustees honored his request for a new

---

building, and he was allowed to hire an assistant teacher. Ten years later, Corbin had a staff of five teachers and an average enrollment of 250 students.

The southern Democratic politicians could not deny Corbin's success. In 1887, the Democratic governor of Arkansas, in his message to the state legislature, talked of "the efficient and faithful management" of Branch Normal College. He referred to Corbin as "an able and efficient principal of that school, devoted to its interests, successful in its management."

Still, despite his success, Corbin endured hostility from the Democratic state legislature simply because he was a Republican. In 1893, the university's board of trustees ignored the state legislature's recommendation that Corbin be fired. Instead, they transferred his managerial duties to a White man, William S. Harris, the college's industrial shops foreman. Corbin stayed on, faithful to the school's mission.

However, in 1902, the board of trustees finally surrendered to the pressures of the state legislature and fired Corbin, replacing him with a young Black, Isaac Fisher, a graduate of Tuskegee Institute in Alabama. Corbin appealed the decision of his forced retirement, but lost. Although he left the college, Corbin's career was not over. He became principal of Merrill High School in Pine Bluff. In 1902, he also served a year as President of the state's Colored Teachers Association and spearheaded the construction of a masonic temple in the city.

When Joseph C. Corbin died in Pine Bluff in 1911, he was survived by two of his six children. Corbin had ridden the tide of Black political success in the Reconstruction Era only to have his career repeatedly jeopardized by White Democrats returning to power in the South. After each disappointment, Corbin bounced back and continued to teach. No one could rob him of his intellectual brilliance in mathematics as well as languages. His mathematical articles and solutions were published in many magazines. Through it all, Corbin was acclaimed as one of the most intellectual men of his race.

WILLIAM H. CROGMAN
(1841-1931)

Orphaned at age 12, and a sailor at age 14, William H. Crogman hardly seemed destined for the life of a noted classical scholar. Yet, this was the fate of this young man, who was to receive no formal education until he was 25 years old.

William was born on May 5, 1841, on St. Martin Island in the Caribbean. Early in life, as a parentless youngster, he was befriended by a White New England shipowner, B. L. Bloomer, who took him into his home in Middleboro, Massachusetts. When he was 14, William joined the crew of one of Bloomer's ships and spent 11 years sailing to many parts of the world.

Crogman returned to Middleboro when he was 25, and Bloomer urged him to add a formal education to the knowledge he had acquired in his travels. In 1868, Crogman entered Pierce Academy in Middleboro, where he completed the four-year academic course in two years. After graduation, he was hired by the Claflin University in Orangeburg, South Carolina, as its first Black instructor of English. But the dream of learning Greek and Latin lured Crogman away from Claflin after only three years. In 1873, he enrolled in Atlanta University for a four-year course in the classics, which he completed in three years.

In 1876, after graduation, Crogman began his long tenure as a classics professor and President of Clark College in Atlanta. He married an Atlanta University graduate, Lavinia C. Mott, and they had seven children. In 1903, Crogman resigned his professorship to undertake the presidency of Clark, becoming the first Black to head the college.

In 1910, however, he resigned to return to his true professional love, the classroom. Both his knowledge and his enthusiasm made him a popular teacher. These qualities also placed Crogman in demand as a public speaker. Twice, he was invited to speak from the pulpit of the Rev. Henry Ward Beecher, the most popular preacher of the day, and pastor of Plymouth Church in Brooklyn.

The educational controversy of the latter 19th Century was the issue of vocational education versus academic courses for Black students. Crogman's position was one that mixed conviction with tolerance. During his tenure as President of Clark, vocational education courses were dropped from the curriculum. He strongly opposed the huge sums of money being given to vocational schools, like Tuskegee Institute, at the expense of liberal arts colleges. But, he recognized the need for Tuskegee and its role in preparing young Blacks for jobs.

When a large exhibit depicting Black progress was assembled for the Cotton States Exposition in Atlanta, in 1895, Crogman was largely responsible for its excellence. Ironically, it was at this exposition that Booker T. Washington catapulted to fame with his praise of vocational education for Blacks. Crogman's attitude toward Southern discrimination was less tolerant, and he would walk several miles from town to campus because he refused to ride on Atlanta's segregated streetcars.

Crogman was an active Methodist. Three times he attended the General Conference of the Methodist Church as a lay delegate, and he was the first Black elected as an assistant secretary for the Conference. In 1892, he became one of fifteen Methodists who set national standards for all Methodist colleges.

William H. Crogman retired in 1922 and moved to Philadelphia, Pennsylvania, where he died on October 16, 1931. He had spent a half century as an educator. He also had fulfilled the earlier prophecy of a contemporary writer who decades earlier described Crogman as "a poor boy cast out upon the world in early life," who had "reached a high position, achieving for himself a position in the hearts of the people worthy of emulation, respect, and honor."

E. FRANKLIN FRAZIER
(1894 - 1962)

The dehumanizing effects of racial segregation were exposed to the world in the writings of Dr. Edward Franklin Frazier. This esteemed educator and sociologist devoted his life to the study of racial problems as his way of combating the human destruction caused by racial prejudice.

Edward Franklin Frazier was born on September 24, 1894 in Baltimore, Maryland, to James and Hattie Frazier. His parents, who lacked an opportunity for formal education, stressed the value of schooling to their five children. Edward attended Baltimore public schools until enrolling in Howard University in Washington, D.C., in 1912, where he distinguished himself in mathematics, literature, and languages.

After graduating, *cum laude*, in 1916, Frazier spent a year teaching mathematics at Tuskegee Institute in Alabama. He also spent a year teaching English and history at St. Paul Normal and Industrial School in Lawrenceville, Virginia, and a year teaching mathematics at Baltimore High School. In 1920, he received a master's degree in sociology from Clark University in Worcester, Massachusetts, and won a research fellowship from the New York School of Social Work to study rural high schools in Denmark.

Returning to the United States in 1922, Frazier married Marie Brown and began teaching sociology at Morehouse College in Atlanta. In 1924, he became Director of the Atlanta School of Social Work. Frazier then began writing on a variety of race-related topics and the role of social work in addressing those issues. One article, "The Pathology of Race Prejudice," published in 1927, so angered Whites in Atlanta that Frazier had to leave the city. From 1927 to 1929, he studied sociology at the University of Chicago, receiving a doctorate in 1931.

After working as research professor of sociology at Fisk University in Nashville, Tennessee, Dr. Frazier joined Howard

University as professor and head of the Sociology Department. In 1940, he received a Guggenheim Fellowship to study in Brazil and the West Indies, and the John Anisfield Award for his book, *The Negro Family in the United* States. Frazier's book traced the history of the Black family in the United States, from the days of slavery, in such problem areas as education, housing, business, and industry. One book reviewer commented, "Few studies have done as much to illuminate the obscure processes of social change as this thorough-going treatment." It was one of several books written by Dr. Frazier, including *Negro Youth at the Crossroads* in 1940, *The Negro in the United States* in 1949, *Black Bourgeoisie: The Rise of a New Middle Class* in 1957, and numerous magazine articles.

Dr. Frazier's *Black Bourgeoisie* was criticized by middle-class Blacks, whose lives were the subject of the book, and whom Frazier accused of trying "to escape identification with the Black masses." Dr. Frazier replied that the book was based on "stark objectivity." His courage in facing criticism surfaced again when he presided over a dinner in New York City honoring W.E.B. DuBois, under indictment as a Soviet agent during the cold War hysteria after World War II. DuBois, who was later acquitted, had been one of Dr. Frazier's mentors.

Dr. Frazier retired as professor emeritus of sociology at Howard in 1959, but continued to teach in the university's Program of African Studies. He also taught at the Johns Hopkins School of Advanced International Studies until his death from a heart attack on May 17, 1962 in Washington, D.C.

Dr. Edward Franklin Frazier's life brought him prestige and many honorary degrees. He was the first honorary Phi Beta Kappa member at Howard and the first Black to head the American Sociological Society. He lectured at the University of London, the University of Liverpool, and the University of Edinburgh. Dr. Frazier prided himself on his efforts to support his absolute opposition to any form of racial segregation.

LESLIE PICKNEY HILL
(1880 -1960)

Remembering what it was like to be poor, Leslie Pickney Hill shared the rewards of his success with young and needy Blacks. This renown scholar and educator thereby claimed an even more important distinction, that of humanitarian.

Soon after Hill's birth on May 14, 1880 in Lynchburg, Virginia, his parents, Sarah and Samuel Hill, moved to Orange, New Jersey. As a young boy, Hill was a talented musician and an excellent student. He might have chosen music as his life's work, but he won a scholarship to Harvard University in Cambridge, Massachusetts. To continue his education, Hill worked many hours as a waiter in the campus dining rooms. However, his academic work did not suffer as a result, and he found the time to be a member of the debating team. In 1903, he graduated, *cum laude*, and was a Phi Beta Kappa member.

In 1904, Hill earned his master's degree from Harvard and went to Tuskegee Institute in Alabama as Director of the Education Department. In 1907, he married Jane E. Clark, Tuskegee's dean of women. In 1910, he joined the Manassas Institute in Virginia as a financial advisor, leaving there in 1913, for a school whose growth he would guide for many years. Hill became principal of the Institute for Colored Youth (ICY), which had several buildings and fewer than two dozen high school students.

Under Hill's presidency, the ICY became Cheyney Training School for Teachers in 1933, taking its name from its location in Cheyney, Pennsylvania. When he retired in 1951 as president emeritus, Cheyney had become an accredited state-supported teachers college with 16 buildings and almost 90 graduating seniors.

Hill's writing versatility was demonstrated in his volume of poems, entitled *Wrongs of* Oppression, published in 1927, and the critically-acclaimed *Toussaint L'Ouverture, A Dramatic History*, written in 1928, with 35 different scenes in five acts. Two of his best-known poems were *The Teacher*, which was translated into several languages and set to music, and *Christmas at Melrose*, which describes his love for his wife and their six daughters.

Hill's humanitarianism took various forms. As director of the Cheyney Chorus, he served as an unofficial ambassador of interracial goodwill when the group toured college campuses. As a writer, he turned over the proceeds of his 1931 biblical drama *Jethro* to a fund for needy students. Then, in 1944, he founded Camp Hope in Delaware County, Pennsylvania, for underprivileged Black youths.

Hill was founder of the Association of Pennsylvania Teachers. He also served as a visiting lecturer at the University of California in Los Angeles. During World War II, his influence was at its peak, and he was a member of the National Education Association Commission of the Defense of Democracy Through Education. In a 1944 wartime publication, *What the Negro Wants*, Hill contributed an essay that called war "the common foe of the whole human race ... a heinous and blasphemous negation of all human relations."

Referring to the Black experience in America, he wrote, "Our democracy is not yet a satisfying reality, but Negroes are still free to live, strive, and die, to make it come in God's unhurried time. All else by comparison is trivial." As a member of the Republican Party, Hill endorsed these party goals for Blacks: equal legal and educational rights, equal access to health care facilities, equal voting rights, and equal job opportunities.

Leslie Pickney Hill died on February 15, 1960, just before the activism of the modern civil rights movement. His death occurred at the Mercy-Douglass Hospital in Philadelphia, where he had served as an administrator after his retirement. He had made the most of those abilities so evident in his childhood. And, in his steady progress through adulthood, Leslie Pickney Hill took time on his journey to help others follow in his footsteps.

JOHN HOPE
(1868 -1936)

Our country's largest Black educational center, the Atlanta University system in Georgia, was the fulfilled dream of John Hope, who struggled for his education on borrowed money and a scholarship. This aristocratic and reserved leader touched the life of virtually every Black intellectual of his day, and he was called "a builder of men" by the famous Black historian Carter G. Woodson.

John Hope was born on June 2, 1868, in Augusta, Georgia, to James Hope, a Scottish immigrant whose wealth allowed him to live openly with John's mother, Mary Frances (Fanny), a child of mixed union. Fanny, however, had no legal claim on James Hope's estate and received only a small trust fund when he died in 1876. John attended public schools in Augusta and worked in a Black-owned restaurant.

In 1886, with money borrowed from his older brother, John entered Worcester Academy in Massachusetts. He worked as a waiter and found the time for sports, the debating society, and the school newspaper. A scholarship allowed Hope to continue his education at Brown University in Providence, Rhode Island. He was on the college newspaper's editorial board and founded an off-campus literary society. At his 1894 graduation, he was the class orator.

While at Brown University, Hope first came face-to-face with his true allegiances—a loyalty to his race. Light enough to "pass for White," Hope had, however, always declared his Blackness. A newfound awareness of his identity came when he heard a campus speech by John M. Langston, the first Black elected to public office in this country. Although invited by Booker T. Washington to teach at Tuskegee Institute in Alabama, Hope chose to join the faculty at a liberal arts college, Roger Williams University, in Nashville, Tennessee.

Hope's disagreement with Washington's educational philosophy was apparent after Washington's 1895 speech in Atlanta. In an 1896 rebuttal to this speech, Hope told a Nashville debating society for Blacks: "If we are not striving for equality, in heaven's name, for what are we living? I regard it as cowardly and dishonest for any of our colored men to tell White people or colored people that we are not struggling for equality..."

Two years later, Hope left Nashville for the Atlanta Baptist College, where he added coaching football to his schedule of teaching the classics. With him, he brought his Chicago-born wife, Lugenia Burns. The couple would later have two sons. In 1906, Hope became the first Black president of the Atlanta Baptist College, which was renamed the Morehouse College in 1913.

Hope made several trips to Europe and became active in many organizations. He served on the board of the NAACP and the National Urban League. He also was President of the National Association of Teachers of Colored Schools and was very active in the YMCA.

Hope's primary legacy, however, was the unification of the Black college-level schools in Atlanta. This was achieved in 1929, by the affiliation of Morehouse, Atlanta University, and Spelman College, creating a system for Black education under Hope's presidency. Clark and Morris Brown colleges and the Gammon Theological Seminary were later added to the system. Among the famous Blacks involved with Hope in this educational crusade were W.E.B. DuBois, Mercer Cook, Robert Russa Moton, Mordecai W. Johnson, E. Franklin Frazier, and Benjamin E. Mays.

On June 20, 1936, John Hope died from pneumonia. After funeral services in the Morehouse Chapel, his body was carried by student pallbearers to a grave site below his office. Countless young Blacks have benefited from the fulfilled dream of a man who advised Blacks: "Be discontented. Be dissatisfied ... Be as restless as the tempestuous billows on the boundless sea. Let your discontent break mount-high against the wall of prejudice, and swamp it to the very foundation."

CHARLES SPURGEON JOHNSON
(1893 - 1956)

Born of humble beginnings, Charles Spurgeon Johnson would become a renown scholar, sociologist, and President of Fisk University. Under Johnson's able leadership, Fisk rose to become a highly regarded center of learning.

Charles Spurgeon Johnson was born on July 24, 1893, in Bristol, Virginia, and named in honor of a noted Baptist preacher. His father, Charles Henry Johnson, was also a Baptist minister and an ex-slave whose owner had taught him Latin, Greek, Hebrew, English, and American literature. His mother, Winifred, created hymns from spirituals and work songs that were sung in Bristol for many years.

Charles, the oldest of five children, read many of the literary classics and theology books that were in his father's library. In 1909, he entered Wayland Academy, a Baptist school for Blacks in Richmond, Virginia. As a young boy, he earned money shining shoes. While at Wayland, he worked as a ditch digger, night watchman, and messboy.

In 1916, Johnson attended Virginia Union University in Richmond, graduating in only three years as valedictorian. During college, he had various jobs. Even with his heavy academic and work schedule, he participated in a wide variety of activities. He was a tennis player, baseball and football team manager, debater, college newspaper editor, and student council president. After graduation, Johnson studied on a fellowship at the University of Chicago and served as a director of research and records for the Chicago Urban League until enlisting in the service during World War I.

In July 1919, Johnson, at the time an infantry sergeant-major returning from active duty in France, was in Chicago when the beatings, stabbing, and shootings of Blacks occurred. That same year, Johnson became Associate Executive Secretary of the Chicago Commission on Race Relations, leaving the position two years later to direct research for the National Urban League in New York City. In 1923, he became editor of the League's new magazine, *Opportunity*, which printed the works of many of the Black writers of the Harlem Renaissance.

In 1928, Johnson became a professor and the Director of the Social Sciences Department at Fisk University, in Nashville, Tennessee. In 1946, he was named President of Fisk, becoming the first Black to hold this position. By the time of his inauguration, he was already one of the country's leading Blacks. He recalled a childhood incident that had haunted him into adulthood. When he was a child, he and his mother would sometimes end a shopping trip with a visit to a soda fountain. One day, the store owner told his mother that he could no longer serve them because of their race. The humiliation was so deep and memorable that Johnson publicly recalled it many years later at his inauguration ceremonies.

After World War II, Dr. Johnson was one of 26 educators sent to Japan to improve that country's school system. He was the author of many books and articles and belonged to numerous government committees and national organizations. Under his leadership, Fisk developed one of the nation's strongest social science departments, in the field of race relations, and was able to double its educational budget. Dr. Johnson assembled an outstanding faculty at Fisk, enabling the establishment of a Phi Beta Kappa chapter on campus. Closed circuit television instruction was instituted, in addition to an early admissions program for outstanding high school students.

On October 27, 1956, Dr. Charles Spurgeon Johnson died of a heart attack in Louisville, Kentucky, while on his way to New York City for a Fisk board of trustees meeting. He was survived by his wife of 36 years, Marie Antoinette, and four children. Some of Dr. Johnson's famous works included: The Negro in Chicago (1922); *The Negro in American Civilization (1930); Economic Status of the Negro (1933)*; and *The Negro College Graduate (1938)*.

MORDECAI W. JOHNSON
(1890 -1976)

When Mordecai Johnson assumed the presidency of Howard University in 1926, the first Black to do so, Howard consisted of a group of unaccredited departments. When Johnson retired 34 years later, Howard was a fully accredited institution with 10 schools and colleges, including a School of Medicine that produced nearly half of the Black doctors in the United States.

Mordecai was born on January 12, 1890 in Paris, Tennessee, to the Rev. Wyatt Johnson and Carolyn Freeman Johnson. His father worked more than 70 hours a week at a mill. Most of Mordecai's time was, therefore, spent with his mother, who encouraged her only child in his studies. After going to public grade schools in his home town, Mordecai briefly attended Roger Williams University's high school in Nashville until a fire there caused him to transfer to Howe Institute in Memphis. This was the beginning of 25 years of schooling.

In 1911, Johnson earned a B.A. degree from Morehouse College in Atlanta; a second B.A. degree in social sciences from the University of Chicago in 1913; a Bachelor of Divinity degree from Rochester Theological Seminary in 1916; a Master of Theology degree from Harvard University in 1922; and Doctor of Divinity degrees from Howard University in 1923 and Gammon Theological Seminary in 1928. Interspersed with his schooling were periods of teaching and YMCA work, but Dr. Johnson wanted to preach and prepared himself with the best education he could get.

After his marriage to Ann Ethelyn Gardner in 1916, Dr. Johnson became the pastor of the First Baptist Church in Charleston, West Virginia. He was active in the town's civic affairs and helped organize the local branch of the NAACP. During this time, he and his wife had two daughters and three sons. In 1926, after nine years in Charleston, Dr. Johnson was chosen as the first Black President of Howard University in Washington, D.C.

At the time, Howard University was a cluster of independent and unaccredited departments. Although his administrative experience was limited, Dr. Johnson immediately developed a 20-year plan for Howard's future development. Within two years, he was able to get Congress to allocate a yearly appropriation for the university's support. This income was supplemented by money from the Julius Rosenwald Fund and other private sources. The building of Howard University began with new academic buildings, dormitories, and laboratories. The teaching staff was doubled, and teachers' salaries were raised.

Teaching tenure became added security for the faculty, which began submitting scholarly articles for publication. Full accreditation was awarded to the Howard's Law School, the College of Liberal Arts, the College of Dentistry, and the Medical School. Johnson accomplished all this within his first 15 years as president. However, his success was not met without some opposition. In the beginning, department heads clung to their independence and resisted change. Later, a group of Black intellectuals were accused of criticizing Johnson in the hopes of securing college positions resulting from a shake-up. Nevertheless, by the time of Johnson's retirement in 1960, the school had an enrollment of more than 6,000 students and a national reputation for excellence.

Many honorary degrees were awarded to Dr. Mordecai W. Johnson, including the NAACP's Spingarn Medal in 1929. Dr. Johnson died, at the age of 86, in Washington, D.C. on September 10, 1976. In 1941, a Howard Charter Day Tribute to Dr. Johnson cited: "You have instituted and developed democratic practices in the internal administration of the University, and in the face of criticism and pressure and at great personal sacrifice, you have at Howard University maintained academic freedom—the very life blood of a university in a democracy."

LUCY CRAFT LANEY
(1854 -1933)

Lucy Craft Laney decided to do something about "ignorance with its inseparable companions, shame and crime and prejudice." She had little money but a great deal of optimism when she embarked on the idealistic, but difficult goal of opening a school for Blacks in Augusta, Georgia, in the 1880s.

Lucy was born in 1854, in Macon, Georgia, the seventh of ten children. Her father, David Laney, was a carpenter and minister who had purchased his freedom and that of his wife, Louisa. Lucy attended high school in Macon and was able to enter Atlanta University with funds from the American Missionary Association.

After graduating in 1873, Laney spent 10 years teaching in various Georgia towns until she gained an opportunity to realize her dream, a chance to open her own school, with help from the Presbyterian Church's Board of Missions for Freedmen. Her first classes were held in a basement room of the Christ Presbyterian Church in Augusta. In 1886, the school received a state charter and was named in honor of Francina E.H. Haines, who helped raise the contributions necessary to keep the school in operation.

What Laney sacrificed for her Haines Normal and Industrial Institute was described by one historian: "She begged and borrowed, paying back when she could ... [She] lived on almost nothing, wearing her shoes until they had no soles, and her hats until they were no longer stylish, shivering through cold nights with too few blankets, even denying herself adequate food, all for the sake of her boys and girls."

Haines Institute prepared young Blacks for college level work and for teaching positions in Black schools. It also gave instruction in home and craft industries and held elementary level classes. One testimonial to its success came from the President of the United States. After spending several months in the South, in 1908, President William Howard Taft told some Hampton Institute supporters at a Carnegie Hall meeting that he "had seen nothing in the way of efficiency and self-sacrifice that could compare with the work of Lucy Laney at Haines Institute." By 1931, the school had 27 teachers, 413 elementary pupils, and about 300 high school students.

In 1890, Laney also opened Augusta's first kindergarten, and in 1892, a nurses' training program that grew into a hospital school of nursing. She took summer courses at the University of Chicago and was awarded master of arts degrees from Lincoln University, Atlanta University, Howard University, and South Carolina State College.

Many a future leader passed through her school's door. Mary McLeod Bethune began her teaching career at Haines. John Hope received "his first love of the classics" from Laney. Laney was interested in the education of women, and saw Black women as "the regenerative force to uplift the Black race." She blamed slavery for robbing Blacks of "the basic rock of all true culture, the home."

The Haines Institute was weakened by the great economic Depression of the 1930s. Private contributions decreased to a trickle, and the church stopped its support. The opening of public schools in Augusta may also be attributed to the Institute's decline, and the school closed in 1949. But, the sacrifice and success of Lucy Laney are not forgotten. Her portrait still hangs in the Georgia State House in Atlanta.

Suffering from high blood pressure and kidney disease, Lucy Craft Laney died on October 23, 1933. Some 5,000 people were said to have passed by her coffin. An Augusta newspaper printed the obituary: "Lucy Laney was great because she loved people. She believed all God's children had wings, though some of the wings are weak and have never been tried. She could see in the most backward that divine personality which she endeavored to coax into flame."

BENJAMIN E. MAYS
(1895-1984)

The Rev. Martin Luther King Jr., called Benjamin E. Mays "my spiritual advisor." Like King, Mays was a man of exceptional qualities—a minister, a scholar, and a recipient of 43 honorary degrees. An authority on Black religion, Mays also spent 27 years as President of Morehouse College, guiding it to a reputation as "the Black Oxford of the South."

Benjamin E. Mays was born on August 1, 1895, the last of seven children born to S. Hezekiah and Louvenia Carter Mays, ex-slaves living in Epworth, South Carolina. From the beginning, he was a bright student, graduating in only three years as the high school valedictorian. His success continued at Bates College in Maine, where he was an honor student and a star debater. In 1920, he earned a bachelor's degree, and two years later, he was ordained a Baptist minister.

Mays' first assignment was in Atlanta at the Shiloh Baptist Church, which was near Morehouse College. And, for two years, he taught mathematics at Morehouse. In 1925, he received a master's degree from the University of Chicago and became an English instructor at South Carolina State College. In 1923, his first wife, Ellen Harvin, died following surgery. In 1926, he was appointed Executive Secretary of the Tampa Urban League, and married for the second time. His second wife, Sadie Gray, was a teacher and social worker.

In 1928, he became National Student Secretary for the YMCA and, in 1930, he began a pioneering two-year national study of Black churches for the Institute for Social and Religious Research in New York City. In 1934, Mays was appointed Dean of Religion at Howard University, and he began a period of international travel on behalf of the U.S. In 1935, Mays received a doctorate from the University of Chicago and was inducted into the Phi Beta Kappa at Bates College.

In 1940, Mays' 27-year presidency of Morehouse College began, and his goal for the college was stated in a 1945 radio address: "It will not be sufficient for Morehouse College, for any college, for that matter, to produce clever graduates, men fluent in speech and able to argue their way through; but rather honest men, men who can be trusted in public and private life—men who are sensitive to the wrongs, the sufferings, and the injustices of society and who are willing to accept responsibility for correcting the ills."

As an authority on Black religion, Mays taught the militant view of religion to the Rev. Martin L. King, Jr., and other civil rights leaders. In one of his numerous articles on the Black church, he wrote that the church kept "one tenth of America's population sanely religious in the midst of an environment that is, for the most part, hostile to it." He warned that Blacks, unless allowed to achieve complete citizenship, would become "more irreligious and "more militant" in their efforts for equality.

Mays' opinions appeared not only in many magazines, but also in his books: The *Negro's Church, The Negro's God as Reflected in His Literature,* and his autobiography, *Born to Rebel.* He was in great demand as a speaker and served as a consultant to the Ford Foundation and the U.S. Office of Education.

In 1967, when the Citizen's Crusade Against Poverty established a board of inquiry into hunger and malnutrition in the United States, Mays was a co-chairman. From 1967 to 1981, he was also a member of the Atlanta School Board, becoming its first Black president.

When Dr. Benjamin E. Mays died on March 28, 1984 in Atlanta, he had witnessed the realization of many of his lifetime goals, including better education, legal and voting rights for his people. Dr. Mays is credited with the inspiration he instilled in many of his students, which included Dr. Martin Luther King, Jr., former mayor Andrew Young, and former state senator Julian Bond.

KELLY MILLER
(1863-1939)

A poor rural family of ten children spawned a man who earned a national reputation as an intellectual leader, educator, and essayist. This son of a slave became so involved with Howard University that the school was commonly called "Kelly Miller's University."

Kelly Miller was born on July 18, 1863, in Winnsboro, South Carolina, and was named for his father, a free Black veteran of the Civil War. He was the sixth of ten children born to Elizabeth Roberts Miller, a slave. While attending a local school, Kelly showed such exceptional mathematical ability that a Presbyterian missionary took interest in him and helped him enroll in a Winnsboro church school in 1878. Two years later, Miller won a scholarship to Howard University's college preparatory school, where he studied mathematics, Latin, and Greek, and finished the three-year course in only two years.

Miller continued at Howard, in the college division, graduating in 1886. He later said of his college experience that it was "difficult to overestimate the advantage of such cultural contact to a country boy of the crude surroundings and contacts such as I sustained prior to my entrance to Howard University." Remembering these roots and with money saved working as a government clerk, Miller bought a farm for his parents as a graduation gift.

After graduation, Miller stayed on at a job in the U.S. Pension Office. An acquaintance of Simon Newcomb, a prominent astronomer and professor of mathematics at Johns Hopkins University, led to Miller's admission as the first Black student at Hopkins. From 1887 to 1889, he took courses in mathematics, physics, and astronomy at the Baltimore campus, quitting when he could no longer afford to attend.

In 1890, after a few months of teaching in a Washington, D.C. school, Miller was hired as a mathematics professor at

Howard University. Four years later, he married Annie May Butler, a teacher at Baltimore Normal School, whom he had met while attending Johns Hopkins. The couple eventually had five children.

Miller became interested in the new academic discipline called sociology, as a means of understanding the American racial problem. In 1895, he was in the educational forefront, when he added sociology classes to Howard's curriculum. He also taught mathematics until 1907, when he chose to concentrate solely on sociology. Miller headed the university's Sociology Department from 1915 to 1925, and taught until his retirement in 1934. He also modernized the College of Arts and Sciences, and was a pioneer in the effort to get Howard to set up a Black Studies program.

Writing and lecturing made Miller a national personality. In the controversy over vocational versus academic instruction for Blacks, Miller criticized both sides as extremists. He called Booker T. Washington, an advocate of vocational education, "lamblike, meek, and submissive." He called Washington's foe, W.E.B. DuBois, an agitator with "an extravagance of feeling and a fiasco of thought." Saying that both forms of education were needed, Miller advocated a comprehensive educational system that would offer a variety of answers to a variety of needs.

He gained the reputation as "Philosopher of the Race Question" and the "Sage of the Potomac." Thousands of people read his essays, both in magazines and book form. He was syndicated in more than 100 newspapers and was the author of many pamphlets, one of which sold more than a quarter millon copies.

Kelly Miller died of a heart attack in his home on December 29, 1939, in Washington, D.C. For more than 50 years, his growing reputation as an intellect had not destroyed his farmboy roots. He tended his vegetable and flower gardens, and never owned a fountain pen or a watch. He had friends who could not read as well as those with doctorates. Kelly Miller, known for his "common touch," was a very uncommon man.

ROBERT RUSSA MOTON
(1867 - 1940)

Presidents sought his advice, and universities gave him honorary degrees. Yet, had it not been for the secret lessons conducted by his mother, he might never have learned to read. Even then, his early schooling was so poor that he could not pass Hampton Institute's regular entrance exam. Nevertheless, Robert Russa Moton rose above his early educational handicaps to a position of national prominence.

Shortly after Robert's birth on August 26, 1867, his parents, Booker and Emily Moton, took jobs on the Samuel Vaughn plantation near Farmville, Virginia. It was there that his mother and the Vaughn's youngest daughter taught Robert to read. After several years of working in a Virginia lumber camp, Moton followed his desire for a formal education and arrived at Hampton Institute. However, Moton could not pass the entrance exam and needed a year of night school before receiving permission to attend regular day classes. With determination and hard work, Moton graduated from Hampton in 1890 and became the school's commandant with the title of major.

The following year, he became a close associate of Booker T. Washington, the founder of Tuskegee Institute in Alabama. When Washington died in 1915, Moton was chosen as President of Tuskegee because he shared Washington's philosophy on Black education, and because he had already distinguished himself at Hampton. He also became President of the National Negro Business League, a position he held for more than 20 years.

At the 1912 commencement at Tuskegee, Moton called upon the graduates to "grasp firmly" three goals: 1) race consciousness, 2) a high moral ideal, and 3) intelligent industry. Moton, like Washington, believed industrial training was the surest road to racial equality. Interracial cooperation was his major method of operation when he worked alongside the

White establishment. These beliefs, which were identical to Washington's, also made him controversial.

Moton's persuasive approach gave him access to many White leaders who would listen to his opinions on racial matters. He served on various presidential commissions and offered advice to the following Presidents: Woodrow Wilson, Warren Harding; Calvin Coolidge; Herbert Hoover; and Franklin Roosevelt. Typical of Moton's approach was his request to President Wilson after the race riots of 1919. He suggested the President "make a statement regarding mob law, laying special stress on lynching and every form of injustice and unfairness." Always politically astute, Moton added; "You would lose nothing by specifically referring to the lynching record of the past six months ... and it would be easy to do it now because of the two most recent riots in the North..."

Every Black in the country praised Moton for his strength in a battle over the staffing of the new veterans' hospital for Blacks at Tuskegee. During 1923 and 1924, great pressure was applied on Moton to staff the hospital with White doctors, White nurses, and Black aides. But even threats from the Ku Klux Klan would not stop Moton from staffing the hospital completely with Blacks. Moton's greatest achievement was the growth of Tuskegee under his direction. During the 20 years of his leadership, until his retirement in 1935, the endowment of the school more than tripled to almost $8 million, and many academic courses were added.

Following the death of his first wife, Moton, in 1908, married Jennie Dee Booth, a Hampton graduate and teacher. They had three daughters and two sons. Throughout his life, and until his death on May 31, 1940, Moton held only two jobs, 25 years as Commandant at Hampton, and 20 years as President of Tuskegee.

Robert Russa Moton's achievements were recognized by his receiving honorary degrees from Harvard University, Oberlin College, Wilberforce University, and Howard University. He was also named recipient of the Harmon Award in 1930, for his contribution to better race relations, and the NAACP's Spingarn Medal in 1932, for distinguished service.

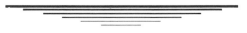

■ FREDERICK DOUGLASS PATTERSON ■
(1901-1988)

Orphaned at the age of two, Frederick Douglass Patterson was not a very likely candidate for fame. But, his determined efforts to obtain a quality education, followed by his genuine concern for Black youths, brought him such success that he was twice honored by the President of the United States.

Frederick was born on October 10, 1901, in Washington, D.C., and was named for the anti-slavery leader Frederick Douglass. The death of his parents, William and Mamie, sent him to live with his sister, Wilhelmina, a schoolteacher in Texas. After four years of study at Prairie View State College in Texas, Patterson entered Iowa State College where he received a doctorate in veterinary science in 1923, and a master of science degree in 1927.

In 1923, Dr Patterson became a teacher in veterinary science and chemistry at Virginia State College in Petersburg, where he was named Director of Agriculture in 1927. The following year, Dr. Patterson was hired by the Tuskegee Institute in Alabama to direct its veterinary department and teach bacteriology. In 1932, he earned another doctorate from Cornell University in Ithaca, New York. He was promoted to Director of Tuskegee's School of Agriculture in 1933, and President of Tuskegee in 1935. He succeeded the Institute's second president, Robert R. Moton, whose daughter Dr. Paterson married in 1935. This marriage produced a son, Frederick.

During Dr. Patterson's tenure as president until 1953, Tuskegee grew in prestige, developing new programs such as a Nutrition Institute to train nutritionists in conjunction with the school's lunch program. He also founded the George Washington Carver Foundation that awarded food science research grants to students. In Dr. Patterson's words, Tuskegee's goal was "to maintain a realistic approach to life's problems by preparing young people not merely to do a specific job well, but to develop in them the spirit of leadership and resourcefulness."

Because of its leadership position, Tuskegee frequently received letters from other schools that sought ways to raise money. Dr. Patterson's interest in this problem led to his founding, and susequent presidency, of the United Negro College Fund (UNCF) in 1944. The UNCF began with 27 member colleges, 12,000 students, and an income of $765,000. Upon Dr. Patterson's death in 1988, the UNCF had grown to 42 member colleges, 45,000 students, and an income of $42 million. The UNCF, whose motto is, "A mind is a terrible thing to waste," is the largest independent source of money for the nation's private Black colleges. It provides staff salaries, student scholarships, laboratory and library resources, and new teaching programs.

From 1953 to 1970, Dr. Patterson was president and trustee of the Phelps-Stokes Fund, which worked for improved status of Blacks in the United States and Africa; the welfare of American Indians; and better low-income housing in New York City. During the 1970s, Dr. Patterson started a new concept for college funding, the College Endowment Funding Plan, which encourages private businesses to donate money to be matched by federal funds. For this plan, Dr. Patterson was cited by President Reagan in 1985. The second recognition from the President came in 1987, when Dr. Patterson was awarded the Presidential Medal of Freedom. A recipient of 13 honorary degrees, Dr. Patterson was also the author of numerous articles for scientific and educational journals. In 1976, he co-authored the book *What the Negro Wants*.

On April 26, 1988, Dr. Frederick Douglass Patterson died of a heart attack at his home in New Rochelle, New York. Praise for his accomplishments came from across the nation, including this tribute by Dr. Donald M. Steward, president of the College Board, the National Association of Schools and Colleges: "He was a visionary and pioneer in American higher education and in Black American higher education ... Dr. Patterson believed that education was the best route for Black mobility ... He set a standard that few of us could meet."

WILLIAM PICKENS
(1881-1954)

William Pickens was the child of sharecroppers. Despite this humble beginning, he became a Yale University graduate, a member of Phi Beta Kappa, a teacher of Latin and Greek, a skilled orator, and a renowned civil rights leader.

William was born on January 15, 1881 in Pendleton, South Carolina, the sixth of ten children born to Jacob and Fannie Pickens, two ex-slaves. After many moves, the family settled near Little Rock, Arkansas, where William graduated first in his class from an all-Black high school. He attended Talladega College in Alabama until 1902, when he transferred to Yale University in New Haven, Connecticut. Before his 1904 graduation with a degree in the classics, he became the second Black elected to Yale's Phi Beta Kappa chapter.

From 1904 to 1914, Pickens taught Latin and Greek at Talladega. He then taught languages for a year at Wiley University in Marshall, Texas before joining Morgan College in Baltimore, Maryland, as its first Black dean. Pickens would later become a Vice-President of Morgan College. He also became an accomplished public speaker and was, in Langston Hughes' words, "one of the most popular platform orators in America." During World War I, for example, Pickens frequently lectured on the unequal treatment of Black soldiers.

First on Pickens' list of Black goals was education, so that people "measured by the same standards" would have equal rights and the opportunities to measure up to those standards. Pickens also called for a democracy in which Blacks were accorded equal rights pertaining to employment, politics, and worship.

Througout his teaching years, Pickens also worked with the NAACP, and was one of its most successful recruiters. In 1920, he left Morgan and joined the NAACP to set up new branches and raise money. From 1919 to 1940, he also wrote articles for the Associated Negro Press that appeared in more than 100 Black newspapers. In 1937, he took a year's leave to lecture to Blacks and Whites on Black history and culture. Pickens also lectured on issues concerning the Federal Forum Project, a national group of adult education centers.

In 1941, Pickens directed the Interracial Section of the Treasury Department's Savings Bonds Division. He was selected because of his early support of America's entry into World War II. The government overlooked the fact that Pickens belonged to the Republican Party and was critical of President Franklin D. Roosevelt's poor civil rights record. Under Pickens' leadership, his staff sold Blacks an estimated $1 billion in war bonds to help the war effort. He retired from the Treasury Department in 1950.

In 1954, Pickens and his wife, Minnie, traveled to Europe, the Middle East, and the West Indies. On April 6, 1954, William Pickens died aboard ship off the coast of Jamaica and was buried at sea. Survivors, in addition to his wife, included three grown children. In his lifetime, Pickens received three honorary degrees and wrote a number of books, including: *Abraham Lincoln: Man and Statesman; The Heir of Slaves; Frederick Douglass and the Spirit of Freedom; Fifty Years of Emancipation, Segregation and Discrimination;* and his autobiography, *Bursting Bonds.*

Pickens often told his audiences: "No door of opportunity should be closed to a man on any other ground than that of his individual fitness." In addition to this credo, this former field hand and son of ex-slaves had exceptional foresight. He told White Americans: "We [Black Americans] believe in this [political equality] as much for South Africa as for South Carolina, and we hope that our American nation will not agree with any government, ally or enemy, that is willing to make a peace that will bind the African Negro to political slavery and exploitation."

JOSEPH C. PRICE
(1854 - 1893)

One of the distinguished orators at the 1881 Methodist Ecumenical Conference in London was Joseph C. Price. From his humble beginnings, this son of a slave stood before the eminent church leaders as a peer. This gifted young orator and clergyman was on his way to becoming a noted educator and civil rights advocate.

Price was born on February 10, 1854, in Elizabeth City, North Carolina. His slave father, Charles Dozier, had assured the freedom of his children by marrying a free woman. After Dozier, a skilled carpenter, was sold away, Joseph's mother married David Price, from whom Joseph took his surname.

During the Civil War, the Prices moved further south in North Carolina to New Bern, which was known as a "rendezvous" for free Blacks. Young Joseph was encouraged in his studies, first by the Rev. Thomas Battle, a Sunday School superintendent, then by a day school teacher, Miss Merrick, and later by James W. Hood, who became an A.M.E. bishop.

In 1866, Price attended St. Cyprian School, which was supported by a Boston philanthropic society. This education enabled him to teach school, from 1871 to 1875, in Wilson, North Carolina. Seeking more education, he attended Shaw University in Raleigh, North Carolina, and then Lincoln University in Oxford, Pennsylvania. Price won prizes in college oratory contests and was graduated valedictorian of his 1879 class.

In his senior year, Price began studying theology and was licensed to preach in 1876, becoming a deacon and an elder of the A.M.E. Zion Church. It was as a church delegate to the London Conference, in 1881, that Price was invited on a lecture tour of the British Isles, where he preached on the condition of Blacks in the United States. During his travels, Price raised $10,000, which he added to the contributions received from the

White citizens of Salisbury, North Carolina, a town selected as the site of his new Black college.

In 1882, Price began his school with five students, one building, and about 40 acres. He continued to receive support from the church and from his lecture tours. One particularly successful tour to California, in 1885, brought him aid from the famous philanthropist Leland Stanford. In 1885, the school was named Livingstone College after the famous explorer and missionary in Africa. It became an important liberal arts college in an era when Blacks were offered, primarily, vocational training in such schools as Hampton and Tuskegee Institutes.

As President of Livingstone College, Price gained in reputation as a man of eloquence and determination, acquiring the title "Lion of the Lyceum." In a speech frequently made in the 1880s, Price would ask, "How long can we deny to men their inalienable and constitutional rights, the denial of which they must keenly feel?" Price said, "A compromise that reverses the Declaration of Independence, nullifies the national Constitution, and is contrary to the genius of this republic, ought not to be asked of any race living under the stars and stripes..."

In 1890, Price was elected President of the National Afro-American League and of the National Equal Rights Convention. He was named Chairman of the Citizens' Equal Rights Association of the United States, which advocated good conduct, education, and acquisition of wealth as the route to full citizenship.

On October 25, 1893, Joseph C. Price succumbed to kidney disease and was buried at Livingstone College. He was survived by his widow and four children. His prominence in Salisbury was evident by the inclusion of four of the town's leading White lawyers as pallbearers, and the presence of the mayor and the city council at his funeral. After Price's death at the early age of 40, the mourners included W.E.B. DuBois, who stated that Price's passing prevented Livingstone from becoming a "Black Harvard."

CHARLES L. REASON
(1818 -1893)

Denied a chance to become a minister because of his race, Charles L. Reason turned to teaching as a career. His early disappointment persuaded him to retaliate against racial prejudice by helping fugitive slaves and writing poetry calling for northern Blacks "to battle in a bloodless fight" for the right to vote.

Charles was born on July 21, 1818, to parents who fled the Haitian revolt of the 1790s. Michael and Elizabeth Melville Reason had lived in Haiti during the civil war launched by Black slaves, who demanded the same rights granted to the people of France. This was the same revolt that brought fame to the great slave-revolt leader Toussaint L'Ouverture.

The Reasons fled to New York City and eventually had four children, a daughter and three sons. The daughter, Policarpe, died at age 4 in 1818. All of the sons later attended the African Free School, where Charles was such a good student that, at age 14, he earned money by teaching other students.

Charles' abilities were recognized by the leaders of St. Phillip Church, who sought to sponsor him as a theology student. So, Charles studied in preparation for entering the General Theological Seminary of the Protestant Episcopal Church in New York City. He was, however, rejected because of his race. Reason joined the abolitionist movement in its efforts to help escaped slaves and bring an end to slavery.

Reason served as secretary, lecturer, and authored position papers for numerous groups that struggled not only against the total slavery of the South, but also against the discrimination in the North. Reason also acquired a reputation as a poet, and he used this talent on behalf of the civil rights of Blacks. In 1841, he wrote "The Spirit Voice," a poem invoking men to prove how dear is freedom." His other poems included "Freedom," "Hope and Confidence," and "Silent Thoughts."

In 1849, the New York Central College, in McGrawville, appointed Reason as "Professor of Belles Lettres and of the French Language and Adjutant-Professor of Mathematics." The college upheld the "Doctrine of the Unity, Common Origin, Equality and Brotherhood of the Human Race." In 1852, Reason was named principal of the Institute for Colored Youth in Philadelphia, which had been established in 1839 to train Blacks for manual labor. Abandoning this narrow objective, Reason added both practical and cultural education to the program, and the school grew from 6 to 118 students in three years.

Reason's appeal for equality of educational opportunities were contained in such essays as "Caste School" in 1850, and "The Colored People's Industrial College" in 1854. In the latter essay, Reason's plea for a Black industrial college stated: "The usefulness, the self-respect and self-dependence, the combination of intelligence and handicraft, the accumulations of the materials of wealth, all referable to such an institution, present fair claims to the assistance of the entire American people."

Reason left Philadelphia in 1855 and spent the next 37 years as a teacher and principal at several schools in New York City. He repeatedly was elected a delegate to the board of directors of the Teachers' Association of New York City, and served as chairman of the association's Grammar School Committee. Reason also was co-founder of the Society for the Promotion of Education Among Colored Children. When he retired from teaching at age 72, he had accumulated more service with the New York City school system than any other teacher.

Although known to have married three times, only the name of his last wife, Clorice Esteve, is contained in biographical information. Charles L. Reason was a widower when he died, on August 16, 1893, of kidney and heart failure in New York City. He was a man who suffered the loss of one career because of racial bias, but overcame disappointment by excelling in another profession.

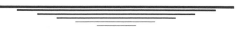

FANNIE MOORE RICHARDS
(1841-1922)

Because she had to receive schooling in secret as a child, Fannie Moore Richards realized the value of an education and devoted her entire life to teaching. For 50 years, she was a public school teacher; and for a longer period, she taught Sunday school.

Fannie was born on October 1, 1841, in Fredericksburg, Virginia. Her father, Adolph Richards, was a native of Guadeloupe, an island near Puerto Rico. Of mixed ancestry and educated in London, Adolph operated a carpentry shop in Fredericksburg. Her mother, Marie Louise Moore, was a native of the town and the daughter of a Scotsman and a free Black woman from Toronto, Canada. The Richards were among the town's free Blacks who operated a secret school in the home of Richard DeBaptiste, and it was there that Fannie received her first schooling.

Fannie's father died when she was only 10 years old. Her mother moved to Detroit, where there were a group of Blacks who had left Virginia for better opportunities in the North. For awhile, Fannie went to school in Toronto, the home of her sister and brother-in-law, and she later returned to Detroit to attend the Teachers Training School.

In 1865, after operating a private school for three years, Fannie Richards was hired as Detroit's first Black public school teacher. Two years later, she and her brother, John, decided to fight Detroit's segregated school system, which gave twelve years of schooling to Whites and only six years of schooling to Blacks. The result was a legal struggle that went all the way to the State Supreme Court and ended the discriminatory policy toward Black children.

Although Richards had fought the school board on the racial issue, she was retained as one of only three Black teachers in the city. She was assigned to the Everett School, where her students were mainly German, Jewish, and a few

Blacks. Richards was popular with both the students and her fellow teachers, and she claimed she never felt "the least discrimination" while on the job.

Richards believed that education was the ultimate key to Black progress, and that her own career was a perfect example. She often pointed out that only lack of opportunity kept Blacks from realizing their full potential. "No race had advanced more rapidly than ours," she wrote, "and Negroes have not shown all they can do yet."

In 1872, when the school board decided to start Detroit's first kindergarten, Richards was selected as the teacher. During this time, she was active in the Second Baptist Church, the city's oldest Black congregation, where she taught Sunday School for more than 50 years. While involved in the education of youth, Richards saved part of her small salary to help the elderly. In 1897, she founded the Phyllis Wheatley Home for Aged Black Women and served as the Home's first president and, later, as board chairman.

During her life, Richards received many honors for her services to the young and the aged. In 1910, Detroit's daily newspaper printed tributes paid to her by prominent White citizens. When the state legislature decided, in 1915, to organize the Freedmen's Progress Commission, it selected Richards as an honorary vice president. Even long after Fannie Moore Richards' death on February 13, 1922, her contributions were still remembered.

In 1970, her memory was honored at a tea in the Detroit Historical Museum, where her portrait was hung to honor of the city's first Black teacher. In the years prior to her retirement in 1915, she earned the respect and admiration of the city's citizens for her scholarship, her innovative teaching methods, and her rapport with children of all races. This little southern girl, who had to learn her first lessons in hiding, had spent her life passing along her knowledge to generations of young people.

ARTHUR ALPHONSO SCHOMBURG
(1874-1938)

Arthur Alphonso Schomburg rescued a portion of the past that might have been lost forever. He assembled a priceless collection of Black history that is available at the New York City's Public Library even today. "History must restore what slavery took away," wrote Schomburg, the 1927 recipient of the Harmon Award for outstanding work in the field of education.

Schomburg was born on January 24, 1874, in San Juan, Puerto Rico, to Carlos and Mary Schomburg. He attended public schools in Puerto Rico, and St. Thomas College in the Virgin Islands. As he grew into adulthood, Schomburg became interested in the movement to free Puerto Rico and Cuba from Spain. He also began to collect photographs and books about the history of Blacks in Puerto Rico.

In 1891, Schomburg left the island and traveled to New York City in the hope of becoming a lawyer. Although he worked in a law office for five years, he became more interested in working with Black study groups. He also served in top leadership posts in Black Masonic lodges, where he achieved the highest rank of 33rd Degree Mason.

In 1896, Schomburg began teaching Spanish. After Cuba was liberated from Spanish rule in the Spanish-American War of 1898, he toured Central America and various islands in the Caribbean. Along the way, he collected all types of memorabilia relating to Black history. In the early 1900s, he used his research to write pamphlets about the Cuban poet Placido and the island of Haiti. Soon books, pamphlets, manuscripts, and etchings began to accumulate in his home, and his hobby became his passion. "The American Negro must remake his past," he would say, "in order to make his future."

In 1906, Schomburg went to work for the Bankers Trust Company, on Wall Street, in New York. During his 23 years with the company, he rose from messenger to head of the mailing department. In 1911, he was the co-founder of the Negro Society for Historical Research and, in 1922, he was elected president of the American Negro Academy. Whenever he could, at his own expense, Schomburg toured Europe, Latin America, and the United States in his search of Black history.

Schomburg was a celebrated lecturer to Negro groups and a contributing writer to numerous highly influential magazines and newspapers. Some of his noted writings include: *Racial Integrity: A Plea for the Establishment of a Chair of Negro History in Our Schools, Colleges, etc.* (1911); *Economic Contribution by the Negro to America* (1915); and *A Bibliographical Checklist of American Negro Poetry* (1916).

The Carnegie Corporation paid $10,000, in 1926, for Schomburg's collection of thousands of books, manuscripts etchings and pamphlets, which was then turned over to the New York City Public Library. The library continues to grow and attract scholars from around the world. Schomburg generously allowed many writers of the Harlem Renaissance period to use his private research collection. And, the noted historian Kenneth B. Clark acknowledges that, when he was a boy, he was personally influenced by the resourceful time and guidance given to him by Schomburg.

In 1929, Schomburg retired from his job at the Bankers Trust and worked for two years as curator of the Negro Collection, at the Fisk University in Nashville, Tennessee. In 1932, he became curator of the Schomburg collection, assembled at the New York City Public Library. Schomburg held this position until his death on June 10, 1938, in New York City. Married three times, he was survived by his third wife, Elizabeth Green, and all seven of his children.

Arthur A. Schomburg believed that his research established three significant conclusions: 1) Blacks have had to struggle for centuries for their freedom, achievement, and progress; 2) Black geniuses and others of accomplishment were considered exceptions to the rule, thereby robbing the Black race of its proper credit; 3) When you examine the history of the Black race, contrary to general belief, the record shows that the achievements and contributions of the Black race have had a major bearing on the early development of world culture.

EMMETT J. SCOTT
(1873-1957)

The field of education had its Black philosophers, leaders, practitioners, and scholars. Emmett J. Scott's contribution to education was different. He was a businessman and administrator, a man who kept the machinery running behind the scenes.

Scott was born on February 13, 1873 to Horace and Emma Scott in Houston, Texas. In 1887, he enrolled in Wiley College in Marshall, Texas, at the urging of the Rev. Isaiah Scott. He spent three years at Wiley, leaving without a degree. However, years later, Wiley College would honor Scott with an honorary degree for his many achievements. What lured Scott away from school was a reporting job on a White daily newspaper, the *Houston Post*. In 1894, after three years at the *Post*, he founded the *Houston Freeman*, a Black weekly newspaper.

In 1895, Booker T. Washington, founder and President of Tuskegee Institute, spoke at the Atlanta Cotton States Exposition. His comments touched off a national debate over academic versus vocational education for Blacks. Scott agreed with Washington's defense of vocational training and wrote an editorial praising the Atlanta speech. In 1897, Booker T. Washington made a public appearance in Houston, arranged by Scott. Washington was so impressed with Scott that he offered him a job as his private secretary. Scott accepted and arrived at Tuskegee, in Alabama, with his wife, Eleanor.

Scott was so in tune with Washington's thinking that he quickly became a close friend and confidant. During Washington's absences from Tuskegee, Scott was left in command. Often, when Washington was unable to make an appearance, Scott went in his place. He visited many times with Presidents Theodore Roosevelt and William Howard Taft, as Washington's representative. Scott also scoured newspapers for items of interest to Washington, and he represented Tuskegee's interests at political gatherings and meetings of Black organizations. So entwined was Scott with what was known as the "Tuskegee Machine," he was considered a successor to Washington after the latter's death in 1915. When the job went to Robert R. Moton, Scott took an appointment, in 1917, as confidential advisor on Black matters to the Secretary of War.

In 1919, Scott began a nearly 20-year career with Howard University in Washington, D.C. As secretary-treasurer and business manager, he was Howard's most important Black administrator until Mordecai W. Johnson was hired in 1926, as the university's first Black president. Scott remained in his administrative position until 1932, but continued as secretary of Howard until his retirement in 1938. He was active in the Republican Party, enlisting Black support for the presidential election campaigns of Warren Harding, Calvin Coolidge, and Herbert Hoover. In 1941, the party established Scott as a shipbuilder in Chester, Pennsylvania, with government contracts to build ships during World War II.

Scott believed that Black business success and property ownership were the best ways to gain White respect, plus political and civil rights recognition. He was the driving force behind the founding of the National Negro Business League in 1900, and served as its secretary for 15 years. Scott was also a very successful businessman. His investments included the Standard Life Insurance Company, the Bank of Mound Bayou in Mississippi, the Afro-American Realty Company of Harlem, the *Voice of the Negro* magazine, the African Union Company, for trade with Africa, and some small automobile companies. All of his primary business ventures were managed by Blacks and served Black customers.

In 1945, when the shipyard closed at the end of the war, Scott retired to Washington, D.C., where he occasionally indulged in public relations work. On December 12, 1957, Emmett J. Scott died after a long illness and was survived by four of his five children. Booker T. Washington, the man who received all the fame, admitted in one of his books that his work would have been "impossible" without Scott's "constant and painstaking care," and he called Scott's help "invaluable."

BOOKER T. WASHINGTON
(1856-1915)

One day in 1872, a penniless and dirty 16-year-old boy arrived at the Hampton Normal and Agricultural Institute in Virginia. He had walked almost 500 miles to seek an education and escape the coal mines of Malden, West Virginia.

This boy, Booker T. Washington, would grow up to become one of the most powerful Blacks in America. One day, he would dine at the White House with President Theodore Roosevelt, and be invited to tea with Queen Victoria in London. Andrew Carnegie, the millionaire philanthropist, called Washington "one of the most wonderful men living or who ever had lived" and entertained him at the Carnegie Castle in Scotland.

Washington was born a plantation slave on April 5, 1856, in Franklin County, Virginia. His mother, Jane, was the plantation cook, and his father was White. He was named Booker Taliaferro, but he took the name Washington when he enrolled in school. By that time, Booker's mother had married Washington Ferguson, and the family was living in Malden. When he was 9 years old, Booker got a job packing salt. He then worked two years in a coal mine before becoming a houseboy for the mine's owner, Lewis Ruffner. He managed to get the fundamentals of education from Ruffner's wife, and by attending night school. In 1872, Washington entered Hampton Institute.

After graduating with a B.A. degree in 1875, Washington taught at a school in Malden before returning to Hampton, in 1879, to organize a night school. That same year, he received an M.A. degree from Wayland Seminary. In 1881, he was chosen to start a new school similar to Hampton in Tuskegee, Alabama. With only $2,000 for salaries and no land or buildings, Washington went to work to get both students and money. Within seven years, Tuskegee Institute had over 400 students and 540 acres of land.

However, national fame did not come to Washington until his public address at the Cotton States International Exposition in Atlanta, Georgia, on September 18, 1895. Washington felt that if Blacks were to pursue the path of hard work, thrift, self-help, and economic progress, Whites would have a greater acceptance of Blacks. His speech drew a standing ovation from the White audience, and later, his racial philosophy made him one of the most powerful and controversial Blacks in the nation. Many Blacks bristled at his words and called Washington passive to the aggressive pursuit of civil rights. Nevertheless, money for the Institute poured in, along with speaking engagement requests for its founder.

Washington achieved a national prominence rare for any person in Black or White America. His autobiography, *Up From Slavery*, published in 1901, became a national best seller and was translated into many languages. President Theodore Roosevelt consulted with him about presidential appointments and asked his advice on many racial policies. As a result, the school that began in a rural Black church grew to more than 60 buildings and a $3 million endowment by 1915.

Washington married three times and had three children. In 1897, he received an M.A. from Harvard and, in 1901, an L.L.D. from Dartmouth College. In 1945, he was elected to the Hall of Fame of New York University. Washington wrote many essays and speeches, which have been published along with numerous books about his life and teachings.

On November 18, 1915, Booker T. Washington was only 59 when he died of arteriosclerosis, and his funeral was attended by nearly 8,000 people. However, his life had been tainted by the scorn of some within his race. But, he accomplished what he had set out to do, perhaps by the only means open to him.

Late in his life, Washington expressed this hope: "More and more, we must learn to think not in terms of race or color or language or religion or political boundaries, but in terms of humanity."

CROSSWORD PUZZLE

ACROSS

2. "A builder of men"
3. Grandson of explorer
4. Founded Livingstone College
6. Honored by *Time* magazine
9. Collector of Black history
11. Freedom purchased for $125
13. Named for anti-slavery leader
15. Educator of future leaders
16. Mathematician and linguist
17. First Black Pres. of Howard Univ.
18. Humanitarian
19. Veteran New York teacher
20. Led music boycott

DOWN

1. Famed sociologist
2. National women's leader
5. 1932 Spingarn Medal Winner
6. Chicago riot investigator
7. Founder of Tuskegee Institute
8. Businessman and administrator
10. Educated in secret
12. Recipient of 43 honorary degrees
13. Language scholar
14. Orphan and sailor
17. Advocate of Black Studies

Now that you have familiarized yourself with our *Salute to Historic Black Educators* in this tenth series of Empak's Black History publications, this section, in three parts, MATCH, TRUE/FALSE, and MULTIPLE CHOICE/FILL-IN, is designed to help you remember some key points about each notable Black in Education. (Answers on page 32.)

MATCH

I. *Match the column on the right with the column on the left by placing the appropriate alphabetical letter next to the person's name it represents.*

1. Peter Humphries Clark _____
2. Robert Russa Moton _____
3. William Pickens _____
4. Charles Spurgeon Johnson _____
5. Charlotte Hawkins Brown _____
6. E. Franklin Frazier _____
7. Rufus E. Clement _____
8. Hallie Quinn Brown _____

A) Commandant of Hampton Institute
B) First Black President of Fisk University
C) Founder of Palmer Memorial Institute
D) Son of a barber
E) Black suffragette
F) Child of sharecroppers
G) Son of "Mother of the Year"
H) Professor emeritus of sociology

TRUE/FALSE

II. *The True and False statements below are taken from the biographical information given on each Black in Education.*

1. Leslie Pickney Hill founded a camp for underprivileged Blacks. _____
2. Emmett J. Scott was Booker T. Washington's private secretary. _____
3. Joseph C. Corbin never received a college degree. _____
4. Arthur A. Schomburg was the first Black President of Hampton Institute. _____
5. Charles L. Reason wanted to become a minister. _____
6. John Hope became the first Black governor of Georgia. _____
7. William Crogman began his formal schooling at age 25. _____
8. Fanny Moore Richards became the first Black graduate of Harvard University. _____

MULTIPLE CHOICE/FILL-IN

III. *Complete the statements below by dawing a line under the correct name, or by filling in the correct answer which you have read in the biographical sketches.*

1. (Robert Russa Moton, Rufus E. Clement, Booker T. Washington) became nationally known after a 1895 speech.
2. (John Hope, Frederick Douglass Patterson, William Crogman) taught veterinary science and agriculture.
3. _____ was called "my spiritual advisor" by the Rev. Martin Luther King, Jr.
4. _____ was the first Black admitted to Johns Hopkins University.
5. _____ founded Haines Normal and Industrial Institute.
6. (Emmett J. Scott, Mordecai W. Johnson, Fannie Moore Richards) was the Spingarn Medal winner for 1929.
7. (Fanny Jackson Coppin, William Pickens, Arthur Schomburg) eventually became a missionary.
8. _____ died at age 40.

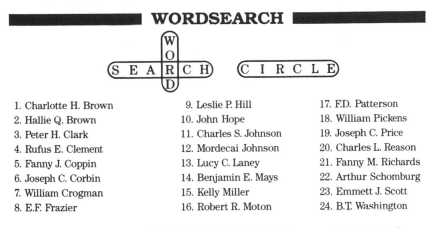

WORDSEARCH

(S E A **R** C H)   (C I R C L E)

W
O
D

1. Charlotte H. Brown
2. Hallie Q. Brown
3. Peter H. Clark
4. Rufus E. Clement
5. Fanny J. Coppin
6. Joseph C. Corbin
7. William Crogman
8. E.F. Frazier

9. Leslie P. Hill
10. John Hope
11. Charles S. Johnson
12. Mordecai Johnson
13. Lucy C. Laney
14. Benjamin E. Mays
15. Kelly Miller
16. Robert R. Moton

17. F.D. Patterson
18. William Pickens
19. Joseph C. Price
20. Charles L. Reason
21. Fanny M. Richards
22. Arthur Schomburg
23. Emmett J. Scott
24. B.T. Washington

The names of our twenty-four HISTORIC BLACK EDUCATORS are contained in the diagram below. Look in the diagram of letters for the names given in the list. Find the names by reading FORWARD, BACKWARDS, UP, DOWN, and DIAGONALLY in a straight line of letters. Each time you find a name in the diagram, circle it in the diagram and cross it off on the list of names. Words often overlap, and letters may be used more than once.

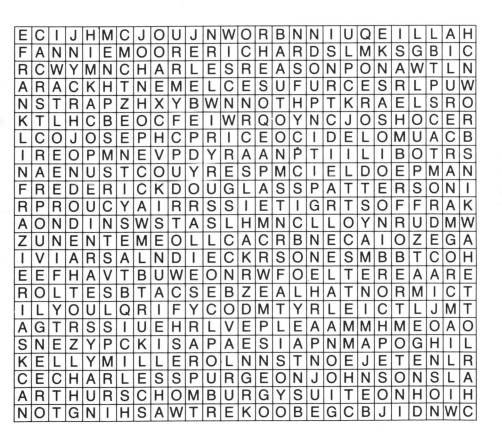

MATCH

1.–D	5.–C
2.–A	6.–H
3.–F	7.–G
4.–B	8.–E

TRUE/FALSE

1.–TRUE	5.–TRUE
2.–TRUE	6.–FALSE
3.–FALSE	7.–TRUE
4.–FALSE	8.–FALSE

MULTIPLE CHOICE/FILL-IN

1.–BOOKER T. WASHINGTON
2.–FREDERICK DOUGLASS PATTERSON
3.–BENJAMIN E. MAYS
4.–KELLY MILLER

5.–LUCY CRAFT LANEY
6.–MORDECAI W. JOHNSON
7.–FANNY JACKSON COPPIN
8.–JOSEPH C. PRICE

CROSSWORD PUZZLE   WORD SEARCH

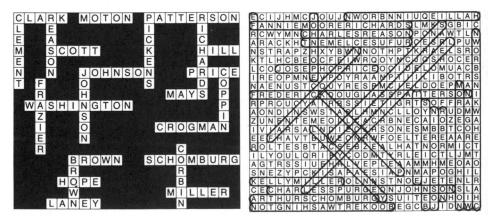

Name _____

Affiliation _____

Address _____
P. O. Box numbers not accepted, street address must appear.

City _____ State _____ Zip _____

Phone# (_____) _____ Date _____

Method Of Payment Enclosed:　( ) Check　　( ) Money Order　　( ) Purchase Order

Prices effective 11/1/95 thru 10/31/96

ADVANCED LEVEL

Quantity	ISBN #	Title Description	Unit Price	Total Price
	0-922162-1-8	"A Salute to Historic Black Women"		
	0-922162-2-6	"A Salute to Black Scientists & Inventors"		
	0-922162-3-4	"A Salute to Black Pioneers"		
	0-922162-4-2	"A Salute to Black Civil Rights Leaders"		
	0-922162-5-0	"A Salute to Historic Black Abolitionists"		
	0-922162-6-9	"A Salute to Historic African Kings & Queens"		
	0-922162-7-7	"A Salute to Historic Black Firsts"		
	0-922162-8-5	"A Salute to Historic Blacks in the Arts"		
	0-922162-9-3	"A Salute to Blacks in the Federal Government"		
	0-922162-14-X	"A Salute to Historic Black Educators"		

INTERMEDIATE LEVEL

	0-922162-75-1	"Historic Black Women"		
	0-922162-76-X	"Black Scientists & Inventors"		
	0-922162-77-8	"Historic Black Pioneers"		
	0-922162-78-6	"Black Civil Rights Leaders"		
	0-922162-80-8	"Historic Black Abolitionists"		
	0-922162-81-6	"Historic African Kings & Queens"		
	0-922162-82-4	"Historic Black Firsts"		
	0-922162-83-2	"Historic Blacks in the Arts"		
	0-922162-84-0	"Blacks in the Federal Government"		
	0-922162-85-9	"Historic Black Educators"		

Total Books		❸ Subtotal	
		❹ IL Residents add 8.75% Sales Tax	
SEE ABOVE CHART	⟶	❺ Shipping & Handling	
GRADE LEVEL: 4th, 5th, 6th		❻ Total	

BOOK PRICING ● QUANTITY DISCOUNTS

Advanced Level	Intermediate Level
Reg. $3.49	Reg. $2.29
Order 50 or More	Order 50 or More
Save 40¢ EACH	Save 20¢ EACH
@ $3.09	@ $2.09

❺ SHIPPING AND HANDLING

Order Total	Add
Under $5.00	$1.50
$5.01-$15.00	$3.00
$15.01-$35.00	$4.50
$35.01-$75.00	$7.00
$75.01-$200.00	10%
Over $201.00	6%

In addition to the above charges, U.S. territories, HI & AK, add $2.00. Canada & Mexico, add $5.00. Other outside U.S., add $20.00.

Name _____

Affiliation _____

Street _____
P. O. Box numbers not accepted, street address must appear.

City _____ State _____ Zip _____

Phone (_____)_____ Date _____

Method Of Payment Enclosed:　　( ) Check　　　　( ) Money Order　　　　( ) Purchase Order

Prices effective 11/1/95 thru 10/31/96

PRIMARY LEVEL... KINDERGARTEN, FIRST, SECOND & THIRD GRADE

Quantity	ISBN #	Title Description	Unit Price	Total Price
	0-922162-90-5	"Kumi and Chanti"		
	0-922162-91-3	"George Washington Carver"		
	0-922162-92-1	"Harriet Tubman"		
	0-922162-93-X	"Jean Baptist DuSable"		
	0-922162-94-8	"Matthew Henson"		
	0-922162-95-6	"Bessie Coleman"		
Total Books			❸ Subtotal	
			❹ IL Residents add 8.75% Sales Tax	
	SEE CHART BELOW ▷		❺ Shipping & Handling	
			❻ Total	

KEY STEPS IN ORDERING

❶ Establish quantity needs.　❹ Add tax, if applicable.
❷ Determine book unit price.　❺ Add shipping &handling.
❸ Determine total cost.　❻ Total amount.

BOOK PRICING ● QUANTITY DISCOUNTS

❶ Quantity Ordered	❷ Unit Price
1-49	$3.49
50 +	$3.09

❺ SHIPPING AND HANDLING

Order Total	Add
Under $5	$1.50
$5.01-$15.00	$3.00
$15.01- $35.00	$4.50
$35.01-$75.00	$7.00
$75.01-$200.00	10%
Over $201.00	6%

In addition to the above charges, U.S. territories, HI & AK, add $2.00. Canada and Mexico, add $5.00. Other outside U.S., add $20.00.

Empak Publishing provides attractive counter and floor displays for retailers and organizations interested in the Heritage book series for resale. Please check here ☐ and include this form with your letterhead and we will send you specific information and our special volume discounts.

- The Empak "Heritage Kids" series provides a basic under-standing and appreciation of Black history which translates to cultural awareness, self-esteem, and ethnic pride within young African-American children.

- Assisted by dynamic and impressive 4-color illustrations, read-ers will be able to relate to the two adorable African kids-- Kumi & Chanti, as they are introduced to the inspirational lives and deeds of significant, historic African-Americans.

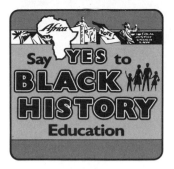

Black History Materials
Available from Empak Publishing

A Salute To Black History Poster Series
African-American Experience–Period Poster Series
Biographical Poster Series
Heritage Kids Poster Series

Advanced Booklet Series
Instructor's Manuals
Advanced Skills Sheets
Black History Bulletin Board Aids
Instructor's Kits

Intermediate Booklet Series
Teacher's Guides
Intermediate Skill Sheets
Black History Flashcards
Intermediate Reading Certificates
Teacher's Kits

Heritage Kids Booklet Series
Heritage Kids Resource & Activity Guides
Heritage Kids Reading Certificates
Heritage Kids Kits

Black History Videos
Black History Month Activity & Resource Guide
African-American Times–A Chronological Record
African-American Discovery Board Game
African-American Clip Art
Black History Mugs
Black Heritage Marble Engraving
Black History Month Banners (18" x 60")
Say YES to Black History Education Sweatshirts
Say YES to Black History Education T-Shirts

To receive your copy of the Empak Publishing Company's
colorful new catalog, please send $2 to cover postage and handling to:

Empak Publishing Company
Catalog Dept., Suite 300
212 East Ohio Street
Chicago, IL 60611